21st Century
Basic Skills
Library

ANIMAL OPPOSITES
SIT AND STAND

by Cecilia Minden

Cherry Lake Publishing • Ann Arbor, Michigan

1

Published in the United States of America
by Cherry Lake Publishing
Ann Arbor, Michigan
www.cherrylakepublishing.com

Reading Adviser: Marla Conn, ReadAbility, Inc.

Photo Credits: © Natalia Barsukova/Shutterstock Images, cover, 20;
© zimmytws/Shutterstock Images, 4; © vvita/Shutterstock Images, 6;
© Henk Bentlage/Shutterstock Images, 8; © Tania Zbrodko/Shutterstock
Images, 10; © AppStock/Shutterstock Images, 12; © GNSKRW/Shutterstock
Images, 14; © BMJ/Shutterstock Images, 16; © image focus/Shutterstock
Images, 18; © MAMZ Images/Shutterstock Images, 20; © marilyn barbone/
Shutterstock Images, 20; © Ksenia Raykova/Shutterstock Images, 20

Library of Congress Cataloging-in-Publication Data
Minden, Cecilia, author.
  Sit and stand / by Cecilia Minden.
    pages cm.—(Animal opposites)
  Audience: K to grade 3.
  Summary: "This Level 1 guided reader illustrates examples of "sitting
and standing" found in the animal kingdom. Students will develop word
recognition and reading skills while learning about opposites and animal
habits."— Provided by publisher.
  ISBN 978-1-63470-475-5 (hardcover)—ISBN 978-1-63470-595-0 (pbk.)—
ISBN 978-1-63470-535-6 (pdf)—ISBN 978-1-63470-655-1 (ebook)
  1. Animals—Juvenile literature. 2. Vocabulary. I. Title.
  QL49.M675 2016
  590—dc23
                                        2015026050

Cherry Lake Publishing would like to acknowledge
the work of the Partnership for 21st Century Skills.
Please visit www.p21.org for more information.

Printed in the United States of America
Corporate Graphics

TABLE OF CONTENTS

What color is the house?

Pets

A cat sits on the step. It waits for its owners to come home.

This is a good trick. The dog is standing up for a treat.

Farm Animals

The little lambs sit next to their mother.

A group of sheep is called a flock. They stand in the **meadow**.

What Do You See?

What pattern is on the tiger's fur?

Zoo Animals

A tiger sits on the log.

An **ostrich** stands on two legs.

Water Animals

A **walrus** has two long teeth.
It sits on the ice.

The **flamingos** stand in the water. They like to stay together.

Which animals are standing?

Which animals are sitting?

Find Out More

BOOK
Horáček, Petr. *Animal Opposites*. Somerville, MA: Candlewick
  Press, 2013.

WEB SITE
The Activity Idea Place—Opposites
www.123child.com/lessonplans/other/opposites.php
Play some games to learn even more opposites.

Glossary

flamingos (fluh-MING-gohs) pink birds with long necks, long legs, and webbed feet

meadow (MED-oh) a grassy field, especially one used for grazing

ostrich (AWS-trich) a large African bird that can run very fast but can't fly

walrus (WAWL-rus) a large sea animal that lives in the Arctic

Home and School Connection

Use this list of words from the book to help your child become a better reader. Word games and writing activities can help beginning readers reinforce literacy skills.

animals	log	step
are	long	teeth
called	meadow	their
color	mother	they
come	next	tiger
farm	ostrich	together
flamingos	owners	treat
flock	pattern	trick
group	pets	two
home	sheep	waits
house	sit	walrus
lambs	sitting	water
legs	stand	what
like	standing	which
little	stay	zoo

Index

About the Author

Cecilia Minden, PhD, is a former classroom teacher and university professor. She now enjoys working as an educational consultant and writer for school and library publications. She has written more than 150 books for children. Cecilia lives in and out, up and down, and fast and slow in McKinney, Texas.